Henri Matisse

Detail from Plate XVI.

Funk & Wagnalls, Inc., New York

JEAN LEYMARIE
TRANSLATED BY RONALD ALLEY

Henri Matisse 1869-1954

Honoured in his own lifetime as one of the great formative masters of twentieth-century art, Matisse had a uniquely full, satisfying career. He was able to devote all of his very long life (he lived to be nearly 85) without interruption to his art. Just as he explored all media with great enthusiasm and success, he explored – and lived in – a variety of locales which provided exactly the right inspiration for his work.

Henri Émile Benoit Matisse, the son of a grain merchant, was born December 31, 1869, in Le Cateau-Cambrésis, a small town in Picardy. After attending school in Saint-Quentin, he was sent, in 1887, to the University of Paris to study law. A year later he was back in Saint-Quentin, clerking in a law office – and taking drawing lessons. It was not until he was twenty-one, while recuperating from appendicitis, that Matisse discovered his true vocation. For want of anything else to do, he began to copy the reproductions in a box of paints his mother had given him, and immediately, as he later recalled, was transported into "a kind of paradise."

In 1891, despite his father's objections, Matisse returned to Paris to study art. Determined to make up for lost time, he "plunged into work 'head down,'" studying first at the Académie Julian under Adolphe Bouguereau, then from 1892 at the École des Beaux-Arts under the Symbolist, Gustave Moreau. He remained there until 1899, on the one hand learning from copying masterpieces in the Louvre (not many modern artists have had so thorough a classical training), on the other hand exchanging ideas with radical young fellow-students such as Georges Rouault, André Derain, Raoul Dufy and Albert Marquet.

It was on a painting trip to Brittany in 1895 that he began to use colour in the Impressionist manner; two years later he exhibited The Dinner Table, *a Renoiresque work, at the Salon de la Société Nationale des Beaux-Arts.*

In 1898 Matisse married Amélie Parayre (they had three children) and went on the first of his many voyages. The couple were away for a year, spent mostly in Corsica, an experience that introduced Matisse to Mediterranean light and colour. Back in Paris, he turned from Impressionism to Pointillism and began to attend evening classes in sculpture. Attracted to the medium by its ability to compensate for the flatness of painting, he eventually produced more than sixty works of sculpture.*

By now a familiar figure in avant-garde circles, Matisse had his first one-man show in June, 1904, at Ambroise Vollard's prestigious gallery. It was a failure. Indeed, the years from 1900 to 1905 were marked by financial crisis – eased slightly by his wife's opening a millinery shop. Meanwhile, however, his stylistic development continued, the influences now being his younger contemporaries Derain, Maurice de Vlaminck and above all Paul Signac, leader of the Neo-Impressionists (or Pointillists). With him, Matisse worked at Saint-Tropez in the summer of 1904, producing, notably, Luxe, calme et volupté, *its title from a poem by Baudelaire, its technique from the Pointillists. The following summer of 1905, spent with Derain at Collioure, a small Mediterranean port near the Spanish border, marked the end of Pointillist influence. One of the results of his new approach to the use of colour was the portrait of Mme. Matisse, painted in Paris later that year.* Woman with the Hat *was exhibited at the 1905 Salon d'Automne in a small cagelike room, along with works by Marquet, Derain, Vlaminck, Rouault and others, all of whom had been painting in violent colours. It was a Paris journalist who dubbed them "les fauves" (wild beasts). Fauvism, never a well-defined movement, soon yielded to the notoriety of Cubism; but Matisse, though a friend of Picasso and Gris, never allied himself with their group.*

1905 was a watershed for Matisse for another reason, too. Leo and Gertrude Stein bought Woman with the Hat, *and from then on the Stein family became Matisse collectors. From 1907 to 1911 he taught at an art school established for him by Sarah Stein and others; in 1908 he exhibited in New York, Moscow and Berlin; in 1909 he* received commissions from a Russian collector, Sergei Shchukin, and signed a contract with the Galerie Bernheim-Jeune in Paris. In 1913 his work was seen again in New York, at the famous Armory Show. The artist's reputation and financial situation were now secure.*

Much of his new wealth was spent on travel: to North Africa – where Islamic motifs attracted his attention and entered his decorative vocabulary, Italy, Russia and later a trip around the world, including Tahiti and the United States. By 1920 Matisse lived mostly in or near Nice. Despite prosperity and international fame his output was unflagging. In addition to painting he returned to sculpture, designed ballet sets and costumes and, in 1932, published twenty-nine etchings illustrating an edition of Mallarmé's Poésies. *Printmaking and drawing had been interests since his early years, but it was not until the outbreak of World War II that he turned actively to book illustration.*

Another of his stylistic shifts was made by Matisse in his late sixties, in 1935. Recognizing a certain slackening of power in his work, he went back to the original Fauvist attempt to "rediscover purity of means" and began to paint flat, patterned motifs with simple contrasts of colour. To the end of his life, in fact, the master's search for new ways of expression continued. Just as in youth he had found his métier while recovering from an illness, so in old age, frequently bedridden, he developed his "papiers découpés," designs cut with scissors from hand-tinted paper. Often he was forced to work on other, larger projects with a crayon attached to a bamboo pole. At the age of eighty-two this man who had once shocked public taste completed what he deemed his masterpiece, the decoration of the Chapel of the Rosary of the Dominican nuns in Vence, a Riviera hill town. From a commission to design stained-glass windows, he had gone on to devise murals, liturgical objects, even clerical vestments. Three years later, on November 3, 1954, Henri Matisse died in his beloved Nice.

"What I dream of is an art of balance, of purity and serenity." —HENRI MATISSE

Painter, sculptor, engraver, decorator, for the whole of the first half of this century Matisse (with Picasso) dominated the artistic scene, on account of the importance of his work and the prestige of his personality. He was already twenty-one years old in 1890, when he suddenly became aware of a vocation of which there had been till then not the slightest intimation; but this enabled him all the better to appreciate the exceptional nature of the turn taken by his destiny.

In 1895 Gustave Moreau recognised his gifts and guided them, telling him prophetically: 'You are going to simplify painting.'

Before mastering colour, Matisse applied himself systematically to the study of tones, variations of light and subject in a sober, restrained colour range. In the Louvre he copied Chardin, Poussin, Ruysdael; he concentrated on still life and intimate composition, to such an extent that on March 12, 1896 his Belgian colleague Evenepoel described him as 'a delicate artist, a master of the art of greys'. It was in this vein that he revealed himself in his first exhibits at the Salon de la Société Nationale and the following year in a large canvas of extreme refinement *La Desserte* (Niarchos Collection, Paris), the final work of his classical apprenticeship. During two consecutive summers at Belle-Ile, he was encouraged by John Russell, who gave him two drawings by Van Gogh, stimulated his interest in colour and introduced him to his friends Pissarro and Rodin. Thanks to their encouragement the pace of his development accelerated unexpectedly. This was the start of an explosion of colour, both instinctive and controlled, which continued until 1901 and which burst forth in the 'impressions' brought back from Corsica and Toulouse, in the views of Arcueil and the Luxembourg sketched in company with Marquet, and in the still lifes seen against the light or viewed looking down from above, and especially in a series of male and female nudes painted with violent expressiveness, as though to liberate himself from every academic convention. The strengthening of his colours led to a corresponding boldness of form, to an incisive assurance of drawing. Matisse moved closer to Cézanne, instinctively attracted by the structure and energy of his painting. From him he learned that the colours in a painting are 'forces' which must be integrated and brought into equilibrium. From 1901 to 1903, the art of Matisse, who was now burdened with the responsibility of a family, passed through a somewhat obscure phase. His wife opened a millinery shop to provide for their necessities, and posed in her spare moments. Matisse worked temporarily on a smaller scale in order to accentuate his volumes and masses and also began to make sculpture under the guidance of Rodin. Experimenting with every kind of expressive means carried to its extreme limit, he aspired to the possession of a complete artistic language. Roger Marx, introducing his first one-man exhibition at Vollard's in June, 1904, praised 'the ruthless demands upon himself' made by the artist and called attention, behind his varied researches, to his obstinate struggle to develop his natural quality as a colourist. This quality revealed itself with revolutionary consequences during his Fauve period (1905-1908), which was preceded by a phase of pointillist transition produced by contact with Signac and Cross. The classic painting of this phase was the one shown at the Salon des Indépendants of 1905, a modern pastoral with a Baudelairean title: *Luxe, calme et volupté* (Private Collection, Paris).

In the summer of 1905 Matisse left for Collioure on the coast of Roussillon, taking with him Vlaminck's usual companion, Derain. There they had as neighbour the collector Daniel de Monfreid, an old friend of Gauguin's to whom they were introduced by Maillol, and who showed them the then still unknown, sumptuous Tahitian pictures. This was a decisive revelation, which occurred at an opportune moment. Matisse gave up pointillist brush-strokes for flat areas of pure colour, creative of space and light. The change was completed in the *Portrait with a Green Stripe* (Plate III), which was exhibited as soon as it was painted at the historic Salon d'Automne of 1905. The painting has this title because of the bold stripe which divides the face into two beneath the hair and which gives it luminosity and relief without recourse to illusionist effects. The colours are situated in clearly distinct zones, and they constitute a harmony made up of dissonance and shock whose intensity is founded on the purity of the elements themselves and on the simplicity of their tension. 'Fauvism was for me', said Matisse, 'an experimentation with means, a way of placing side by side, of combining in an expressive and constructive manner a blue, a red, a green. It was the result of an instinctive need which I felt, and not of a deliberate decision.'

In his second one-man show, held at the Galerie Druet in March, 1906, Matisse exhibited work in a variety of media: drawings, sculpture and a new series of lithographs and woodcuts, as well as paintings. Of greater significance, however, was his monumental composition *La Joie de Vivre* (now in the Barnes Foundation, Merion, Pa.), which was concurrently being shown at the Salon des Indépendants. This painting is an epitome of his art; it is a brilliant synthesis of rhythmic line and areas of unbroken colour,

which reconciles two traditionally contrasting themes, the pastoral and the bacchanalian.

After the opening of the Galerie Druet exhibition, Matisse made his first journey to North Africa, long a centre of attraction for colouristic painters including Delacroix and Renoir. He returned there many times, attracted by the sun and by Islamic art. From a fortnight's stay at Biskra he brought back Arab textiles and ceramics which he used later to embellish his paintings; he returned straight to Collioure, where he remained until the end of the summer. With tireless energy, he produced numerous landscapes, still lifes and figure studies, and carried on his experiments in a variety of directions, now towards massive forms surrounded by bold outlines, now towards flowing and decorative arabesques. The *Still Life with a Red Carpet* (Plate V-VI), the finest of these paintings, combines in its magnificence an extraordinary range of technical procedures. Fauvism at its peak is none other than this free experimentation with colour and drawing carried to its ultimate in economy and expression.

The Salon d'Automne of 1906, which included the largest retrospective exhibition of Gauguin that had ever been organised, was centered around Matisse and the Fauves, who at that time were at the height of their splendour. The basic principles of the movement, which Matisse defined in an important article in the 'Grande Revue', in December, 1908, may be summarised as follows: the equivalence of light and spatial construction through colour, the dominance of flat planes without chiaroscuro or modelling,

1. SELF-PORTRAIT
MUSEUM OF MODERN ART, NEW YORK

2. SEATED NUDE
MUSEUM OF MODERN ART, NEW YORK

purification of the expressive means, complete correspondence between the expression, that is to say the emotional content, and the decoration, that is to say, the order of the composition. 'Composition is the art of arranging in a decorative manner the various elements at the painter's disposal for the expression of his feelings.' Form and content coincide and modify one another through mutual reaction since 'expression comes from the coloured surface which the spectator takes in its entirety'. Born from a spontaneous reaction to colour ('the expressive side of colour affects me in a purely instinctive way'), Fauvism was for Matisse a dynamic sensualism, 'the impact of a scene on the senses', disciplined by synthesis, by 'condensation of the sensations', and subjected to the fundamental economy of painting.

'Every part is visible and must fulfil its allotted role, primary or secondary. That is to say everything which is not useful in a picture is detrimental.' Intensity of colour taken by itself, without this constructional severity and this unity of transposition, is insufficient to characterise the movement. 'It is no more than the external aspect,' said Matisse; 'Fauvism came about because we excluded all imitative colours, and because we obtained more powerful reactions with pure colours — stronger simultaneous reactions; and it was concerned furthermore with the *luminosity* of colours.' It involved therefore, like Gauguin's painting, a completely arbitrary way of using pure colours in flat areas, subject to imagination and not to reality, an ability to create on the picture surface the kind of pure harmony which Matisse called 'spiritual space'. The retrospective exhibition at the Salon d'Automne of 1907 was devoted to Cézanne, whose constructional influence succeeded the decorative one of Gauguin, and Matisse himself was not uninfluenced by this change. In face of the rise of the cubist group led by Picasso, which resulted in the breakup of Fauvism, Matisse continued his luminous explorations on his own, while tightening the construction of his works in response to the new developments. The expressionist intensity and the contrasting tendencies which came together in the course of this year, so crucial in the history of modern art, led to the extraordinary *Pink Nude* (Plate XVI), while the two related versions of *Luxury* (Plate II and Nationalmuseet, Copenhagen) tend towards monumental purification, a harmonious resolution of the relationship between the figures and the background by means of arabesques and planes which are all the more evocative for being simplified. At the Salon d'Automne of 1908, at the moment when he opened an art school of international renown and published a lucid account of his aesthetic views, Matisse took stock of his recent efforts, and, with the exhibition of the decorative panel which he executed for the Russian collector Shchukin (based on a dominant blue that was later changed to red), initiated the magnificent audacities of the following decade.

From 1909 to 1917 Matisse moved away from Paris and went to live at Issy-les-Moulineaux in the neighbourhood of Clamart, in a large peaceful house in the middle of a garden. In this setting and at this period he created his most important works, works whose majestic serenity seems like a victory over disquiet and inner struggles. A visit to an exhibition of Islamic art at Munich in October, 1910, the discovery of icons during a trip to Moscow in November, 1911, long winter stays in Andalusia and Tangier from 1910 to 1913, stimulated a new interest and confirmed his line of development. In reaction against the intimate character of easel painting, he turned to Asiatic and Byzantine models, aspiring after the solemnity of mural compositions which several commissions gave him the opportunity to achieve. In 1911 he completed two panels commissioned by Shchukin, *Dance* and *Music* (now in the Hermitage Museum, Leningrad); restricted to three dominant colours, the blue

3. STUDY REPRODUCED FROM A NOTEBOOK OF PRELIMINARY DRAWINGS FOR 'LA PERRUCHE ET LA SIRÈNE'

of the sky, the red of the figures, the green of the hillside, they embody the universal essence of movement and repose. Also in 1911, he executed for Michael Stein a decoration in tempera, now the pride of the Museum at Grenoble, *Still Life with Eggplants* (Plate VII), dazzling in its profusion of ornamental motifs. The same year the couturier Poiret refused *The Blue Window* (Museum of Modern Art, New York), a hieratic transformation of the view from the artist's bedroom, a symphony of blue offset by the red of a carnation. The magisterial series of *Interiors* begun likewise in 1911 — *The Red Studio* (Museum of Modern Art, New York), *The Painter's Studio* and *The Painter's Family* (Hermitage Museum, Leningrad), with their continuous decorative background — attained its supreme perfection in 1916 with *The Piano Lesson* (Plate VIII) in which the basic tonality is provided by a grey offset by the geometry of the coloured plates. The last of the series of sumptuous canvases inspired by his sojourns in Tangier was painted in 1916. *The Moroccans* (Museum of Modern Art, New York) is a remembered vision of an exotic setting.

In June, 1914, Matisse took a studio in the center of Paris, on the Quai Saint-Michel, to work in during the winter months. Its interior, with a window overlooking the Seine and the Palais de Justice in the background, is recognizable in several paintings, severe in composition and sober in colouration. In contrast is the 1917 *Music Lesson* (Barnes Foundation), a work that evoked, for the last time, the festive atmosphere of the suburban home in Clamart which he was soon to leave forever. The beginning of his now more frequent and protracted stays in the south of France is marked by such dazzling works as *Interior with a Violin* (Plate IX) or the *White Plumes* (Plate X).

Caught up in the mood of relaxation following the war, he turned briefly to a facile and ingratiating style of painting, exemplified in numerous odalisques in a rather self-conscious atmosphere of luxury. In the second half of the 1920's, however, he recovered himself, returning to density of colour and firmness of structure. He also took up sculpture again. The *Odalisque with a Tambourine* (Plate XIII), the *Decorative Figure against an Ornamental Background* (Plate XIV) testify to this renewal of energy which continued without respite.

The visual impressions received during three months spent in Tahiti in 1930 were stored up, to be invoked in works of later years. From the Pacific, Matisse went to the United States, where he served as a member of the jury of the Carnegie International in Pittsburgh and received from the Barnes Foundation a commission to do a mural representing the dance. *Danse II* (the first study on this theme was the decorative panel designed for Shchukin's Moscow residence) was installed by the artist himself after an initial version, unusable because its dimensions were wrong, had been completely reworked. It was also during this period that Matisse made his first major contribution to graphic art: the twenty-nine etchings which with their supple, economic lines perfectly illustrate the poems of Mallarmé (1932).

Initiated in the requirements of mural painting, Matisse tended increasingly towards a decorative treatment, especially in his most successful works, *Pink Nude* (Plate XVI), *Music* (Plate XV) and in the tapestry cartoons made in 1946 and based on Polynesian memories. In 1948, after final masterpieces such as the *Interior with the Egyptian Curtain* (Phillips Collection, Washington) or the *Large Interior in Red* (Plate XI-XII), Matisse deliberately gave up oil painting and easel pictures to invent, when more than eighty years old, techniques which he used in a more and more simplified and striking way. From 1948 to 1951 he concentrated his energies on the Chapel of the Rosary at

Vence, a monumental synthesis for whose design he was entirely responsible: he undertook the architecture as well as decoration, including windows, ceramics and liturgical ornaments. His main object, in his own words, 'was to make a balance between a surface of colours and lights and a flat wall, with black drawing on white'.

From 1950 until his death in 1954, pale drawings in chinese ink alternated with large compositions in gouache and areas of colour cut out with a pair of scissors. Unlike cubist 'papiers collés' or surrealist 'collages', these 'papiers découpés' by Matisse consist of coloured forms indissolubly linked, which are adapted to the mural support by the precision of their relationships and of their arrangements.

Instead of tracing in an imaginary space forms derived from outside, the artist cuts in a pre-existing block of colour, like a sculptor in wood or marble, forms originating from within and consubstantial with the material in which they are inscribed. To achieve such skill, the reward of a lifetime of unremitting hard work, 'it is obviously necessary' — wrote Matisse — 'to have at one's disposal all one's accumulated experience and to know how to preserve the freshness of one's instincts'. Thanks to his recourse to complete simplicity and absolute radiance, Matisse recapitulated and sublimated his entire work, extolling the transparency of clear skies, the flowers and fruits of the earth, the inexhaustible arabesque of the female body, the triumphant disc of the sun, and revived on the verge of death the enchanted visions of Tahiti. Only his mastery of 'papiers découpés' allowed him to evoke the impression of the vast limpid spaces of Polynesia, the iridescence of the lagoons which, he said, are a painter's paradise. An oceanic light irradiated his last compositions, carrying to fulfilment his life-long desire 'to create a crystalline abode for the spirit'.

4. SEATED NUDE WITH ARMS FOLDED
METROPOLITAN MUSEUM OF ART, NEW YORK

I. A STUDY FOR 'JOIE DE VIVRE' (1905)
Oil on canvas. 18⅛ in. x 21⅝ in.
Nationalmuseet, Copenhagen

This is the first of three preparatory oil sketches for a large canvas shown at the 1905 Salon d'Automne. It was to this painting, and other works exhibited by Matisse and his friends, that the description 'fauvist' (like a wild beast) was first applied. The study for the finished painting, done while Matisse was staying in Collioure in the summer of 1905, is suffused with vivid colour and still shows touches of pointillist technique. But the regular, close dots of paint (*pointillés*) have become strokes, alternating with ribbons of flat colour which thread through the composition.

No human figures appear, although they are incorporated in the painting in its final form. Here Matisse is primarily concerned with the expressive use of colour to depict pure landscape; and his determination to free himself from rendering forms and colours naturalistically enhances its idyllic quality. In the tree trunks, the foliage and along the ground we see the artist's short, seemingly random brush strokes conveying the cheerful animation of the scene. On the right, the foliage is green, with vibrant contrasts of orange and violet suggesting the brightness and shading within the leafy areas. The curving tree trunks—sinuous verticals in many tones of blue, green, violet and red—create a surface of pulsing rhythms.

II. LE LUXE (LUXURY) I (1907)
Oil on canvas. 82¾ in. x 54⅜ in.
Musée Nationale d'Art Moderne, Paris

Allusions to classical myth underlie Matisse's variation on the theme of Venus rising from the sea. She stands, the personification of *luxe*, naked and carefree, being helped out of her discarded drapery by an attendant. Another rushes up to present a bouquet of flowers.

Matisse often did pairs of paintings, the first treatment of the subject being generally freer, more tentative and naturalistic, the later one an abstract refinement. Such is the case here; in fact, Matisse himself labelled this earlier version an 'esquisse' (sketch). The main figure is decisively outlined, her form and features and the pearly lustre of her flesh indicated. But line and colour in the other figures is, in comparison, indecisive. The long, graceful curve of the crouching woman's body, for example, is merely silhouetted against the sandy shore.

Alternate bands of warm and cool tones, rapidly brushed in irregular strokes, stand for shore and sea, and hills and sky beyond. There is a monumental simplicity to these landscape forms, in harmony with the treatment of the larger than life-size human figures which, though statuesque, are in no way sculptural.

III. PORTRAIT WITH A GREEN STRIPE (1905)
Oil on canvas. 16 in. x 12¾ in.
Nationalmuseet, Copenhagen

This portrait of the artist's wife is typically Fauvist in its seemingly arbitrary, actually structural, use of colours. Matisse was concerned not with psychological portrayal but with the possibilities of colour as a means of defining human form. In this he goes beyond Gauguin or Van Gogh in their daring attempts to reveal character.

No face is completely symmetrical. The artist, realizing this, has painted the shadowed half in yellow ochre with green outlines; the left side, in the light, is pink outlined with rose. A green line—the hue complementary to the natural pink in skin tones—divides the facial planes. At the same time it also saves the face from being overwhelmed by the strong background colours.

Behind Mme Matisse's head, on her right, warm shades of violet and orange-red counteract the cool ochre in her face; conversely, to her left, greens complement the warmer tone of that half of the face. The patchy painting of this varicoloured background gives an effect of areas of stained glass—united by the mass of blue-black hair. Black is used throughout in short, random bursts to unify the form, emphatically outlining one ear, the chin, shoulders, part of the collar.

IV. STILL LIFE WITH GOLDFISH (1911)
Oil on canvas. 45¾ in. x 39⅜ in.
Museum of Modern Art, New York

This is the second of six paintings centred about a bowl of goldfish. Here an aquarium, a vase of flowers and a terracotta figurine form a still life arrangement of disparate objects unified by line and colour. The fluidity suggested by the swimming fish is developed in the sinuous curves of the sculpture. (This latter is a representation of one of Matisse's own pieces, *Reclining Nude I*, modelled in 1907.) Fish and flowers are painted in a similar vivid red; fish tank and vase are linked by their blue-green colour, the colour of the water they hold and of the wedge of shadow behind them. The rectangle of light yellow suggesting an open door adds its cool note to the appropriately aqueous tonality.

The still life components are not so much flatly patterned against the translucent sky-blue background as it is painted around them. This can be seen by the strokes of blue paint outlining the hip of the statuette or the top of the small window at the upper right. Narrow white margins of unpainted canvas, sometimes reinforced by black lines, serve to isolate areas of colour and to separate shapes from the abstract background.

V-VI. STILL LIFE WITH A RED CARPET (ORIENTAL RUGS) (1906)
Oil on canvas. 35 in. x 45¾ in.
Musée des Beaux-Arts, Grenoble

In a series of still lifes painted in 1906 and 1907 Matisse repeatedly used the textiles and pottery he had brought back to Collioure from a trip to North Africa. This is a work typical of his Fauve period, bold in its use of pure, strongly contrasted colours. Characteristic also of this phase is the mixture of large, pointillist dots of pigment and patches of flat colour. In certain areas Matisse leaves the canvas bare, in other places employs heavy dark lines to reinforce his drawing, as in the book at the centre or in the rugs heaped up at the right.

Colour is indeed the important element in this painting. To it composition and form—even the patterns of the rugs and the ceramic dishes filled with fruits—are largely subordinated. Only the green gourd and the design motifs in the rug hanging above the table are more than summarily indicated. The objects on the table, seen from above and aslant, lie scattered, unrelated to one another.

VII. STILL LIFE WITH EGGPLANTS (1911–12)
Tempera. 82¾ in. x 96⅜ in.
Musée des Beaux-Arts, Grenoble

At first it seems that Matisse has painted the room, the curtained alcove behind it and the view outside as one flat surface, unified by the abstract floral pattern that dances across floor and walls. On closer study, this complex of verticals, horizontals and squares creates an illusion of space and depth; from the mantelpiece at the left to the gold-framed mirror beside it, the eye is drawn into the room along the folds of the screen. Floor and wall surfaces begin to be differentiated. The slight perspective line of the shutter gives a suggestion of space beyond the window. This landscape view is almost on the same plane as the interior and related to it chromatically. In many other paintings Matisse attempted similarly to link outdoors and indoors, to make natural forms and sunlight a part of interior design.

Small as they are, it is the eggplants—seen as if from above on the low table—that give a central focus. Their simple shape and subdued colour provide a quiet contrast to the other design motifs. Three in number, they correspond to the division of the whole composition into three vertical segments.

Henri-Matisse

VIII. THE PIANO LESSON (1916–17)
Oil on canvas. 96½ in. x 83¾ in.
Museum of Modern Art, New York
(Mrs. Simon Guggenheim Fund)

Contrasts and repetitions of shapes and colours comprise Matisse's witty commentary on a music lesson being given to his son Pierre in the family living room at Issy-les-Moulineaux. The rigidly elongated, grey body of the teacher, authoritatively placed on high, is diametrically opposed (in placing and mood) to the sensuous, warm brown curves of the little nude statue. In actuality, the figure of the teacher is a version of Matisse's own *Woman on a High Stool*, painted in 1913–14; the bronze sculpture is his, too—the *Decorative Figure*, done in 1906.

The stern black pyramid of the metronome is echoed in the triangle that serves to indicate a shadow falling across the boy's face. Both shapes are relieved by another long triangle, a green suggestion of outdoor freedom in a garden below. Delicate, decorative arabesques—the wrought iron of the balcony, the grid of the music-rest—interrupt the tension of the vertical and diagonal lines and the areas of flat colour they demarcate.

Vestiges of Cubist style linger in this essentially geometrical composition of overlapping planes. Depth becomes ambiguous, just as the distinction between the real world and the world of painted or sculptured forms becomes blurred.

IX. INTERIOR WITH A VIOLIN (1917–18)
Oil on canvas. 45¾ in. x 35 in.
Nationalmuseet, Copenhagen
(J. Rump Collection)

Matisse's love of music dictated the theme of many of his paintings. Here, his special fondness for the violin has been expressed by the contrasts between its shape and the severely geometrical black and white pattern of the room, between its warm reddish-brown tone and the blue of the case in which it is enshrined. This beautiful blue, softly glowing in the shadowed room, is the keynote of the composition, linking inside with outside. Its cool tonality harmonizes with the lime green of the plant and the light, shining blue of the sea beyond the window. The dark interior, relieved only by glints of sunshine, provides a dramatic background for the instrument and the yellow chair on which it rests.

More than in most of his paintings a sense of depth is conveyed by the line of the casement extending into the room. Dazzling Mediterranean air and light are also important components of the naturalism in this composition. Hinted at through the closed shutter, they are revealed by the open shutter. In the light thus admitted all the colours in the room—yellow, blue and red-browns—are picked up in a prismatic band shimmering on the floor under the window.

X. WHITE PLUMES (1919)
Oil on canvas. 29 in. x 24 in.
Institute of Arts, Minneapolis

For this splendidly patterned portrait of his favourite model, Antoinette, Matisse himself constructed the hat. Fascinated with the expressive possibilities of its shape he made a series of drawings and one other painting of Antoinette wearing it. Here, pictorial excitement comes from striking placements of colours, textures and shapes. The frothy, pearl-white ostrich plumes are set off by the dense richness of the red background and by the woman's jet black hair, hardly distinguishable from the loops of black and white ribbon hanging down from the hat. The red of her lips and the touch of black at her waist provide colour keys to the whole composition, at the same time enlivening the monochrome effect of skin tone and dress. The simplicity of this colour scheme is effectively dramatic.

The magnificent sweep of the feathers enhances the severe Latin beauty of the model, echoing the pronounced curves of her eyebrows and the almond shape of her eyes. Shadows playing around these grave eyes repeat the larger shadow seen under the hat brim. At the same time, visual interest is added by the contrast between the arabesque of the feather trim and the angular V-shaped top of the dress.

XI-XII. LARGE INTERIOR IN RED (1948)
Oil on canvas. 57½ in. x 38¾ in.
Musée Nationale d'Art Moderne, Paris

Of a series of interiors painted in 1947–48, this is acknowledged to be the masterpiece. It is, in fact, of all his paintings the one Matisse himself considered his best. He has achieved here an 'absolute' red that links foreground and background, floor and walls, in one colour plane. The absolute simplicity, too, of this composition lies in the balanced repetition of a small number of objects: vases of flowers and a plant, two pictures of floral subjects (representations of Matisse's own works), two tables, two animal skins on the floor. These are disposed symmetrically on either side of the black line that halves the canvas vertically.

The tables stand side by side, separated by a bench which, in its stark black squareness, provides a contrast to the curves of the table legs and the floor coverings. Above each table hangs the picture appropriate to it. The sketchy black and white drawing is placed over the white-topped table; the denser masses in the painting—of a pineapple—correspond to the more substantial forms below it. Again, the pervasive tonality works to balance and link the essentially black and white left side with the stronger, more colourful right-hand side.

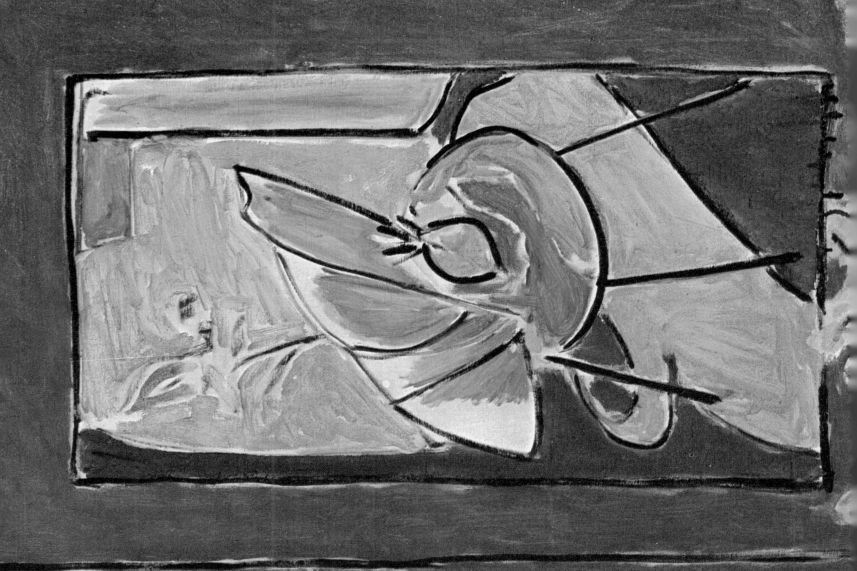

XIII. ODALISQUE WITH A TAMBOURINE (1926)
Oil on canvas. 28 in. x 21 in.
Collection of Mr. William S. Paley, New York

One of Matisse's many paintings of voluptuously posed nudes, this reaffirms his interest in the theme of the odalisque, stimulated by his first trip to Algeria years before. North African light and mood pervade this canvas, from the rectangle of Mediterranean blue seen through the window and the dazzling sunshine filtering into the shuttered room, to the glowing colours and patterned walls revealed by this light. The red of the carpet, with its suggestion of Oriental lushness, is contrasted with the vivid green in the chair—its striped pattern also recalling certain Near Eastern textile patterns. And the red is repeated on the edge of the tambourine at the upper right, accenting its oval shape. This is also the shape of the woman's head, to which attention is particularly called by the arm curved over it.

In the same way the yellow stripes seem to vibrate against the green of the chair covering, strong glints of light on the woman's body serve to emphasize its volumes, in contrast to the mauve and grey shadows delineating its planes. These shadows, like the rug, stand out against the rest of the painting because of their drier, crustier, more impasted surfaces.

XIV. DECORATIVE FIGURE AGAINST AN
ORNAMENTAL BACKGROUND (1927)
Oil on canvas. 51½ in. x 38¾ in.
Musée Nationale d'Art Moderne, Paris

This work is the culmination of Matisse's preoccupation with the female nude in an Oriental setting. Here he paints the model almost as a sculptured figure, the rosy tones in the shadowed planes of her body harmonizing with the soft background colour of the wallpaper and the warm reds in the rug. Except for this, however, her form is in strong contrast to the rococo wallpaper design and the Oriental rug pattern.

The folds of drapery that wrap about her torso, like the broad, dark outline of her head and shoulder at the left and like the exaggerated columnar straightness of her neck and side, all serve to detach her from her lush surroundings. This opposition of object to background creates vigourous, dynamic tensions among all elements of the composition. By contrast, however, the green leaves of the plant contained within a blue and white pot are almost organically integrated with this background. The shape of the leaves conforms on the right to the curve of the decorative framework in the wallpaper design; on the left they blend into the painted wallpaper leaves.

XV. MUSIC (1939)
Oil on canvas. 45¼ in. x 45¼ in.
Albright-Knox Art Gallery, Buffalo

A series of photographs records the development of this painting, showing how Matisse changed the position of the musician, placing her higher and higher, eventually integrating her figure with the background motif, and how he gradually simplified the composition. Where originally the women were counterpoised, the sweeping curves of their bodies now repeat one another, despite differences in costume and colour. These curves of hip and thigh are echoed by the shape of the guitar, so that the player and her instrument almost become one. Thus a figural harmony is achieved, appropriate to the subject. The work takes its place with those other compositions built around a stringed instrument—or a piano—showing the artist's great love of music. Another kind of calming harmony is evoked by the unbroken frieze of enormous philodendron leaves marching rhythmically across the top. This marks one of Matisse's earliest uses of leaf shapes as a decorative background motif.

Pure pattern, this work has been constructed with great linear clarity, in the manner of the neoclassic painter Ingres, whom Matisse so admired. Solid outlines isolate each colour area and define the forms and figures, in a manner reminiscent of the much earlier *Luxe* (Plate II).

XVI. PINK NUDE (1935)
Oil on canvas. 26 in. x 36½ in.
Museum of Art, Baltimore
(Cone Collection)

Matisse documented this work in progress over a six-month period by twenty-one photographs that show how he slowly simplified and exaggerated the model's proportions to create a monumental decorative composition. Gradually, his use of colour became flatter and he made the checked surfaces of background and foreground more geometric to offset the sinuous curves of the figure. The woman's right elbow and left hand extend out of the picture frame, as do her feet. This design device expands the figure to fill the whole picture space and creates a rhythmic flow balancing the severe angularity of her couch and the window behind it. The shocking pink and red stripes cut by her left knee offer a contrast in colour as well as in line to the form of her body. Matisse's preoccupation with dynamic tensions in all his later ornamental works is shown in the complex balance here between plain and patterned surfaces, between rest and movement, and between warm flesh colour and the blue of the sofa cover.